Adventures in GREATER PUGET SOUND

WRITTEN BY
DAWN ASHBACH

ILLUSTRATED BY
JANICE VEAL

NORTHWEST ISLAND ASSOCIATES
ANACORTES, WASHINGTON

www.NorthwestIslandAssociates.com

Copyright ©1991 Dawn Ashbach and Janice Veal. Revised edition 2011.
Library of Congress Catalog Card Number 91-62044 • ISBN 0-9629778-0-2 • Printed in the United States of America.

CETACEANS

Whales may look like fish but they really are mammals. Mammals are *warm-blooded*, nurse their babies, breathe air through their lungs, have some hair and have a backbone. Whales, dolphins and porpoises belong to a subgroup of the mammal order called *Cetaceans*.

Whales are the largest

Mother orca and her young

mammals to have lived on Earth. They are so heavy they need to live in the water to support their weight and avoid crushing themselves to death. Whales, dolphins and porpoises have a blanket of fat, called *blubber*, that helps them float. Blubber also helps keep them warm and acts as a food source.

ARMS AND FLIPPERS

Instead of arms, cetaceans have flippers. Compare the bones of the whale's flipper to the human arm and hand. What does this show you about whales and humans?

Draw a line matching 8 of the whale bones to 8 of the human bones. One has been done for you.

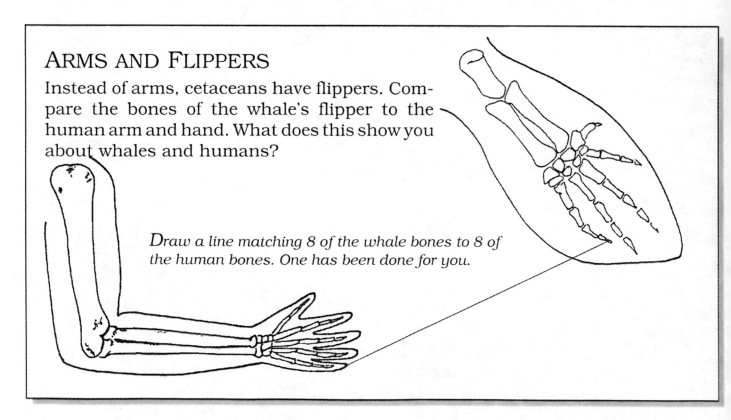

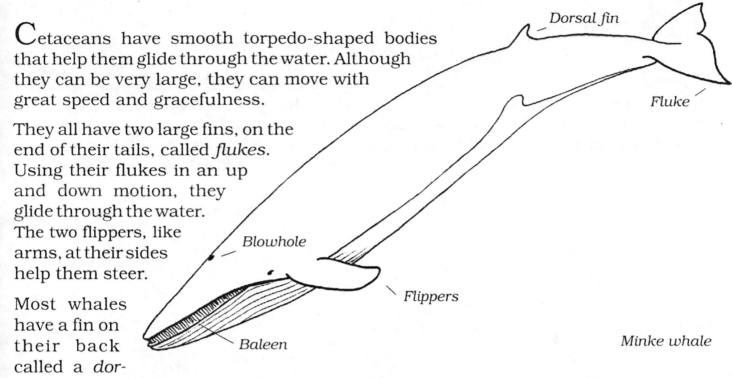

Cetaceans have smooth torpedo-shaped bodies that help them glide through the water. Although they can be very large, they can move with great speed and gracefulness.

They all have two large fins, on the end of their tails, called *flukes*. Using their flukes in an up and down motion, they glide through the water. The two flippers, like arms, at their sides help them steer.

Most whales have a fin on their back called a *dorsal fin*, which helps them stay balanced. Their nostrils, called *blowholes*, are on top of their head. Some cetaceans have teeth and some have *baleen*.

Dorsal fin

Fluke

Blowhole

Flippers

Baleen

Minke whale

Unscramble the words and discover different parts of a cetacean's body. Word list: flipper, lungs, blubber, hair, dorsal, flukes, blowhole and baleen.

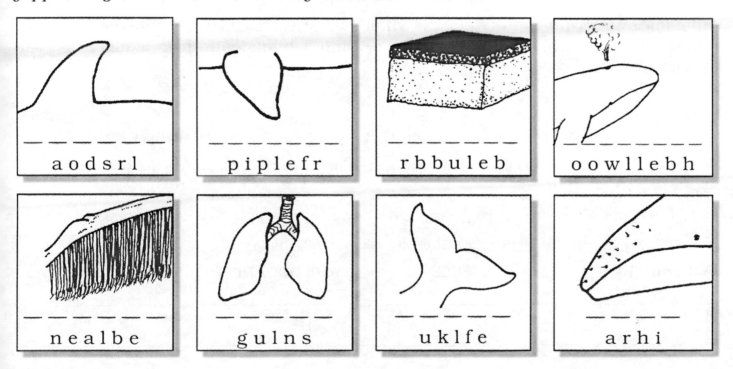

a o d s r l

p i p l e f r

r b b u l e b

o o w l l e b h

n e a l b e

g u l n s

u k l f e

a r h i

3

BLOWHOLES

Cetaceans have a special method of breathing. Unlike fish, they have no gills through which to extract oxygen from the water. Instead, they have lungs and hold their breath while under the water and must return to the surface for air. Their nostrils are located on top of their heads and are called blowholes. Baleen whales have two blowholes on the top of their head and toothed whales have one.

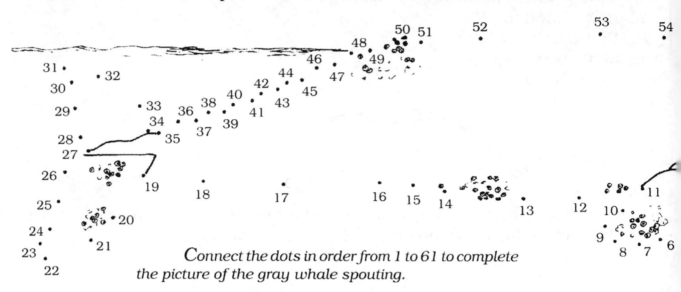

Connect the dots in order from 1 to 61 to complete the picture of the gray whale spouting.

As they surface, they have about two seconds to open their blowholes to quickly breath out the used air and take in approximately 2,000 quarts of fresh air. Some whales can hold their breath for as long as 75 minutes.

Spouting or *blowing* occurs when the whale's breath is released through the blowhole. Moisture in the whale's breath condenses into white steam. It is like seeing your breath on a cold day.

Find out what early whalers shouted when they spotted a spouting whale.

Circle the letter in each row that is different. Write it in the box below that has the same number as the row.

1 FFFTFFFFF

2. NNHNNNN

3. HHHAHHH

4. BBBBBRB

5. CCCCSCC

6. EEEEEHE

7. FEFFFFFF

8. PPPBPPPP

9. DLDDDDDD

10. QQQOQQQ

11. XXWXXXX

12. ZZZSZZZZ

1	2	3	4	5	6	7	8	9	10	11	12

WHALING

Baleen whales were almost made extinct before the introduction of plastic because baleen was used for many things, such as women's corsets, umbrella ribs, knitting needles, jewelry and brushes. Whales were also hunted for use in making candles, soaps, cosmetics, perfumes, pharmaceuticals, paints, many kinds of oils and lubricants, animal feed, fertilizers, detergents and art objects. Thanks to conservation efforts many endangered whales are making a steady comeback.

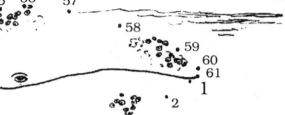

HIDDEN PICTURE

In the picture below, can you find 11 products made from whales? Find the bar of soap, knitting needles, candle, umbrella, necklace, comb, pet food, scrimshaw, oil lamp, perfume bottle and paint can.

WHALE BEHAVIORS

Whales, dolphins and porpoises are sometimes seen leaping clear out of the water. This behavior is called *breaching*. It can occur for several reasons. When they hit the water, the impact forces irritating crustaceans and parasites to fall off their body. They may breach to observe the area around them and sometimes just for fun.

Spy hopping occurs when a cetacean looks like it is treading water. They use their muscular tails, called *flukes*, to lift their heads out of the water to check out the surroundings.

Fluke smacking or *lob-tailing* is a method of long distance communication between individuals or groups of cetaceans. The sound of their slapping the water carries for miles and can sound like a cannon blast.

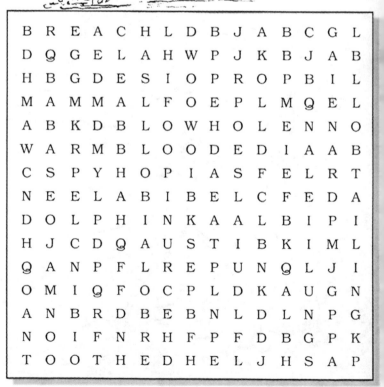

Whales, dolphins and porpoises share many common things.

Look across, up, down, backwards and diagonally to find the 18 words listed below. Circle the words.

Baleen
Blowhole
Blubber
Breach
Cetacean
Dolphin
DorsalFin
Flipper
Flukes
Lobtailing

Lungs
Mammal
Porpoise
SpyHop
Toothed
WarmBlooded
Whale
Hair

B	R	E	A	C	H	L	D	B	J	A	B	C	G	L
D	Q	G	E	L	A	H	W	P	J	K	B	J	A	B
H	B	G	D	E	S	I	O	P	R	O	P	B	I	L
M	A	M	M	A	L	F	O	E	P	L	M	Q	E	L
A	B	K	D	B	L	O	W	H	O	L	E	N	N	O
W	A	R	M	B	L	O	O	D	E	D	I	A	A	B
C	S	P	Y	H	O	P	I	A	S	F	E	L	R	T
N	E	E	L	A	B	I	B	E	L	C	F	E	D	A
D	O	L	P	H	I	N	K	A	A	L	B	I	P	I
H	J	C	D	Q	A	U	S	T	I	B	K	I	M	L
Q	A	N	P	F	L	R	E	P	U	N	Q	L	J	I
O	M	I	Q	F	O	C	P	L	D	K	A	U	G	N
A	N	B	R	D	B	E	B	N	L	D	L	N	P	G
N	O	I	F	N	R	H	F	P	F	D	B	G	P	K
T	O	O	T	H	E	D	H	E	L	J	H	S	A	P

BALEEN WHALES

Whales are divided into two groups, *baleen* and *toothed*. The main differences are how and what they eat. Baleen whales have plates of baleen which hang from their upper jaws on either side of their tongue. It looks like a bristly moustache. Baleen, sometimes called *whalebone*, is actually a skin growth, somewhat like fingernails. The inside edge is frayed making a fine mesh which acts as a strainer.

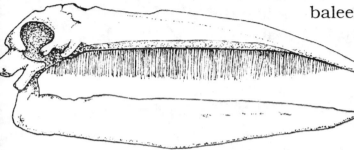

Gray whale skull with baleen plates

Baleen whales eat small plants and animals called plankton. Many of these organisms are so tiny, you need a microscope to see them. Krill, a kind of plankton, is the main food of baleen whales. They are reddish brown shrimp-like animals, about two inches long.

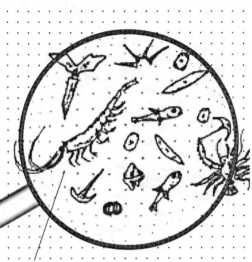

Krill and Plankton (Magnified)

Some baleen whales feed by *skimming* the surface of the water. Other baleen whales feed by opening their mouth and gulping huge amounts of water. Closing their mouth, they use their tongue to push the sea water out through the strainer of whalebone. Plankton, krill, fish and small animals are trapped inside and swallowed whole.

Gray whales, nicknamed "Mussel-diggers", specialize in bottom feeding. They have between 140 to 180 ivory-colored baleen plates hanging from each side of their upper jaw. They use their huge snouts to stir up the ocean bottom and scoop up mouthfuls of mud. Using their tongues, they strain the muddy water through their baleen swallowing tiny plants and animals. They can eat as much as 2,000 pounds of food per day.

Gray whale

GRAY WHALES

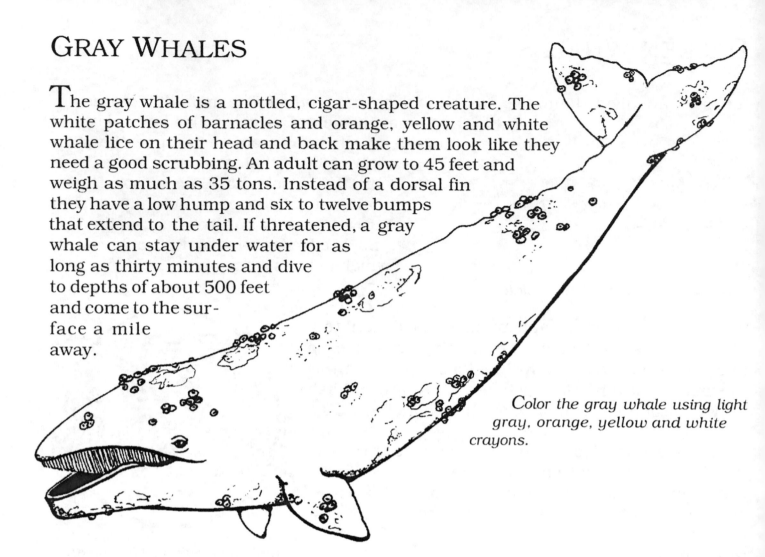

The gray whale is a mottled, cigar-shaped creature. The white patches of barnacles and orange, yellow and white whale lice on their head and back make them look like they need a good scrubbing. An adult can grow to 45 feet and weigh as much as 35 tons. Instead of a dorsal fin they have a low hump and six to twelve bumps that extend to the tail. If threatened, a gray whale can stay under water for as long as thirty minutes and dive to depths of about 500 feet and come to the surface a mile away.

Color the gray whale using light gray, orange, yellow and white crayons.

Did you know that a gray whale's tongue can weigh as much as 3000 pounds!

What can you think of that weighs 3000 pounds?

MIGRATION CALENDAR

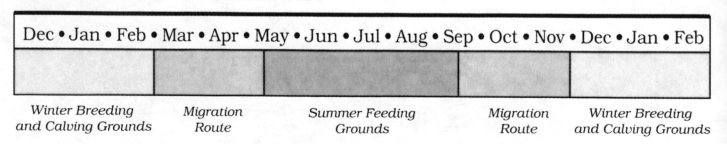

Dec • Jan • Feb • Mar • Apr • May • Jun • Jul • Aug • Sep • Oct • Nov • Dec • Jan • Feb

| Winter Breeding and Calving Grounds | Migration Route | Summer Feeding Grounds | Migration Route | Winter Breeding and Calving Grounds |

8

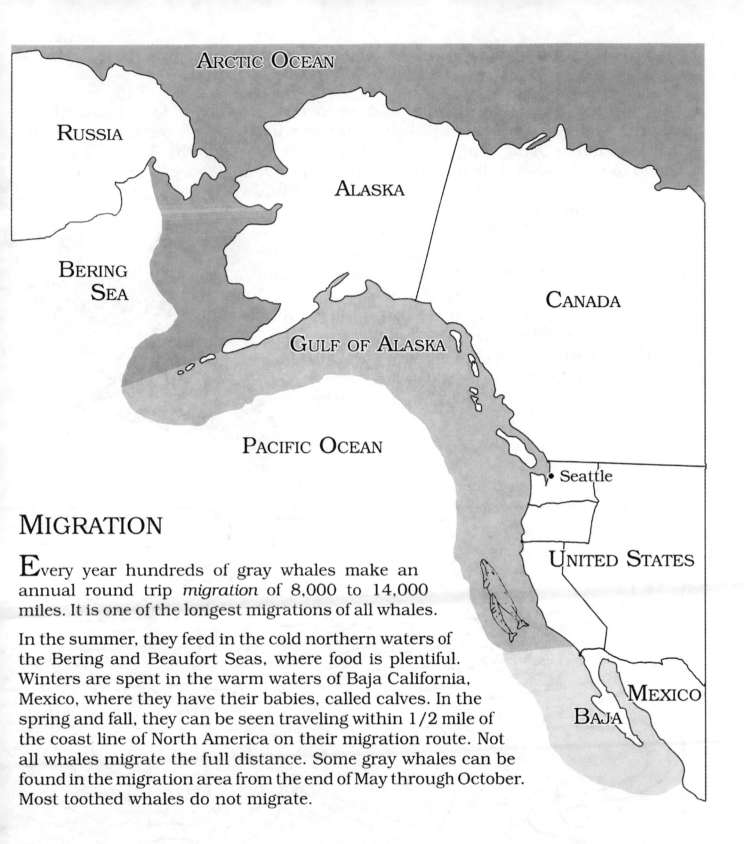

MIGRATION

Every year hundreds of gray whales make an annual round trip *migration* of 8,000 to 14,000 miles. It is one of the longest migrations of all whales.

In the summer, they feed in the cold northern waters of the Bering and Beaufort Seas, where food is plentiful. Winters are spent in the warm waters of Baja California, Mexico, where they have their babies, called calves. In the spring and fall, they can be seen traveling within 1/2 mile of the coast line of North America on their migration route. Not all whales migrate the full distance. Some gray whales can be found in the migration area from the end of May through October. Most toothed whales do not migrate.

In the fall, when the pack ice begins to form over their feeding grounds, the gray whales begin their migration south. Trace the migration route of the whales from their Arctic feeding grounds to the warm waters of Baja.

9

TOOTHED WHALES

Toothed whales include all dolphins and porpoises. They have at least two teeth and hunt prey such as fish, squid and other marine animals. Their teeth are covered with ivory, similar to the enamel on human teeth. Each year a thin layer of ivory is added to each tooth. It is possible to count the layers of ivory to estimate the age of the whale. They use their teeth to capture their prey, then swallow their food whole.

Generally, toothed whales are more socially organized than baleen whales. They live and travel in family groups called *pods* and can be seen cooperating during a hunt. They have a well developed language, using high frequency whistles, clicks, chirps and squeaks to communicate with each other. They are generally smaller than the baleen whales and are faster swimmers.

10

ECHOLOCATION

Most toothed whales use *echolocation* to find their food. When hunting, they make high pitched clicking sounds. The echoes of their clicking help the whales locate their prey. When the sound hits a fish, the echo bounces back to the whale. By listening to the echo, the cetacean can tell the fish's location. Many species of toothed whales do not migrate. Since they generally feed on fish, they spend most of their time in temperate waters, close to shore.

Orcas are called "killer whales" because they feed on marine mammals, fish and even other whales. By hunting in packs with other orcas, they are very successful in catching their prey.

The orca has "spouted" and is ready to take a deep breath. He will close his blow hole before diving. Can you help him find his dinner?

11

ORCAS IN GREATER PUGET SOUND

Whale watching is a favorite activity in Puget Sound and the San Juan Islands. If lucky, you may see an orca. They have black bodies with white undersides and white patches above both eyes. Each orca can be identified by the shape and size of their dorsal fin and the white and gray markings behind and beneath the dorsal called a saddle patch. A female's dorsal averages three feet, a male's can be as tall as six feet. When full grown, males average between 25 and 30 feet long and weigh between 14,000 and 20,000 pounds (about 9 tons). They can travel as fast as 30 miles an hour. Orcas are the largest of the dolphin family and considered the most intelligent.

Use the grid to draw Fluke or Rhapsody. Notice the difference in the height of their dorsal fins. Color your picture.

Fluke, L-105, male (2004)   Rhapsody, J-32, female (1996)

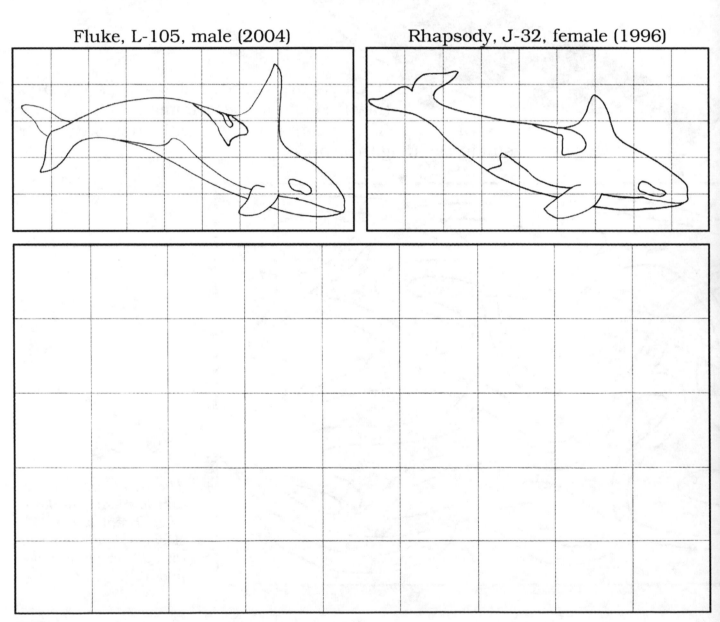

FAMILY PODS

Today there are 88 orcas living in the Southern Resident Community of greater Puget Sound. They travel in three family groups called pods, named J, K and L. Pods are formed around mothers and their babies, some have four generations traveling together. Individuals are given names according to their pod, estimated birth date and sometimes their personalities. Orcas living in the three pods are available for adoption through *The Whale Museum's Orca Adoption Program*. You can find out more at www.whalemuseum.org.

Fluke, L-105
male, born 2004

Samish, J-14
female, born 1974

Blackberry, J-27
male, born 1991

Riptide, J-30
male, born 1995

Echo, J-42
female, born 2007

Slick, J-16
female, born c.1972

Coho, L-108
male, born 2006

Orcas are identified by differences in their dorsal fins and white and gray saddle patches. Can you name these five orcas?

Polaris, J-28
female, born 1993

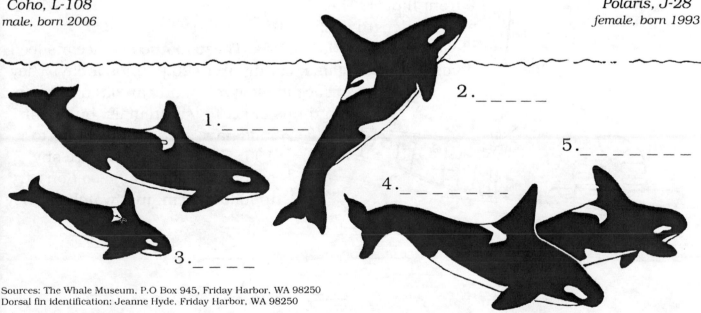

1._ _ _ _ _ _ _

2._ _ _ _ _ _

3._ _ _ _ _

4._ _ _ _ _ _ _

5._ _ _ _ _ _ _

Sources: The Whale Museum, P.O Box 945, Friday Harbor, WA 98250
Dorsal fin identification: Jeanne Hyde, Friday Harbor, WA 98250

MINKE WHALES

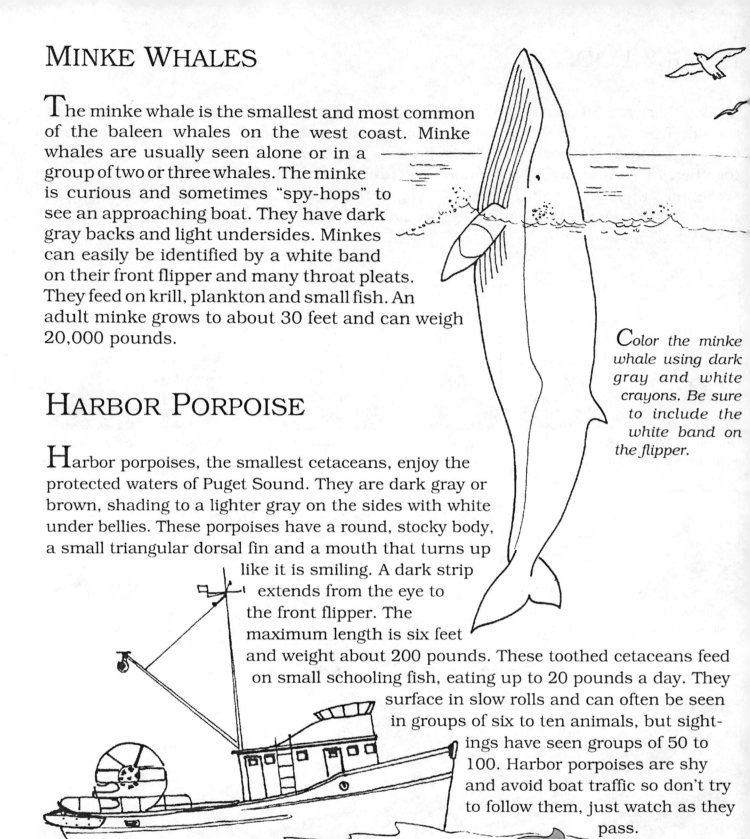

The minke whale is the smallest and most common of the baleen whales on the west coast. Minke whales are usually seen alone or in a group of two or three whales. The minke is curious and sometimes "spy-hops" to see an approaching boat. They have dark gray backs and light undersides. Minkes can easily be identified by a white band on their front flipper and many throat pleats. They feed on krill, plankton and small fish. An adult minke grows to about 30 feet and can weigh 20,000 pounds.

Color the minke whale using dark gray and white crayons. Be sure to include the white band on the flipper.

HARBOR PORPOISE

Harbor porpoises, the smallest cetaceans, enjoy the protected waters of Puget Sound. They are dark gray or brown, shading to a lighter gray on the sides with white under bellies. These porpoises have a round, stocky body, a small triangular dorsal fin and a mouth that turns up like it is smiling. A dark strip extends from the eye to the front flipper. The maximum length is six feet and weight about 200 pounds. These toothed cetaceans feed on small schooling fish, eating up to 20 pounds a day. They surface in slow rolls and can often be seen in groups of six to ten animals, but sightings have seen groups of 50 to 100. Harbor porpoises are shy and avoid boat traffic so don't try to follow them, just watch as they pass.

14

WHALE SCALE

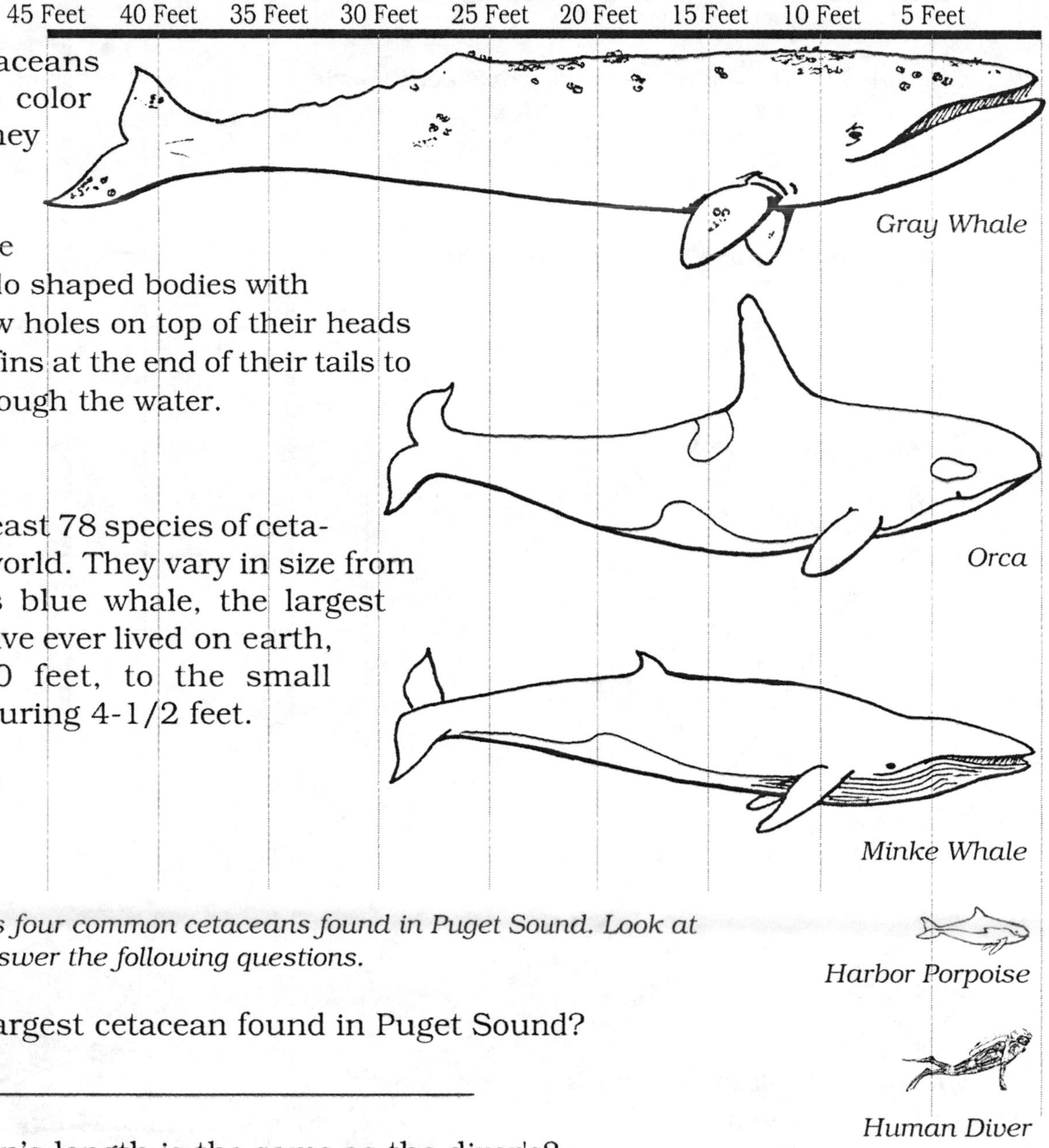

Although cetaceans differ in size, color and habits, they all have some things in common. They have smooth, torpedo shaped bodies with one or two blow holes on top of their heads and large, flat fins at the end of their tails to prpel them through the water.

There are at least 78 species of cetaceans in the world. They vary in size from the enormous blue whale, the largest mammal to have ever lived on earth, measuring 90 feet, to the small vaquita, measuring 4-1/2 feet.

Gray Whale

Orca

Minke Whale

Harbor Porpoise

Human Diver

The scale shows four common cetaceans found in Puget Sound. Look at the scale and answer the following questions.

What is the largest cetacean found in Puget Sound?

_____

What cetacean's length is the same as the diver's?

_____

If the length of a truck is 15 feet, what cetaceans are the length of 2 trucks?

_____   _____

Name the two baleen whales on the scale. _____

Which cetacean has the largest dorsal fin?_____

15

WHALE CROSSWORD

Using the clues below, fill in this whale crossword puzzle.

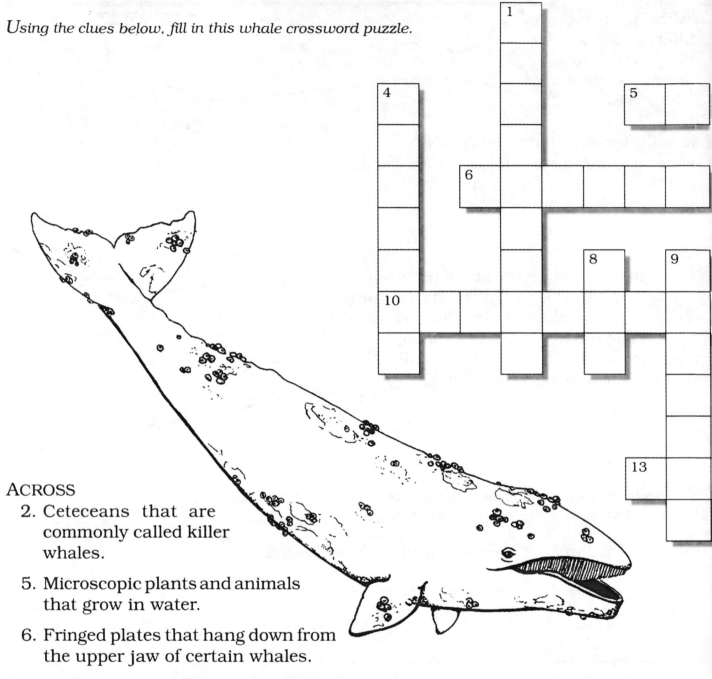

ACROSS

2. Ceteceans that are commonly called killer whales.

5. Microscopic plants and animals that grow in water.

6. Fringed plates that hang down from the upper jaw of certain whales.

10. High-pitched clicking sounds some whales use to find their food.

13. Nostril located on top of the head of ceteceans.

14. The arms of marine mammals that are used for swimming and stabilizing.

16

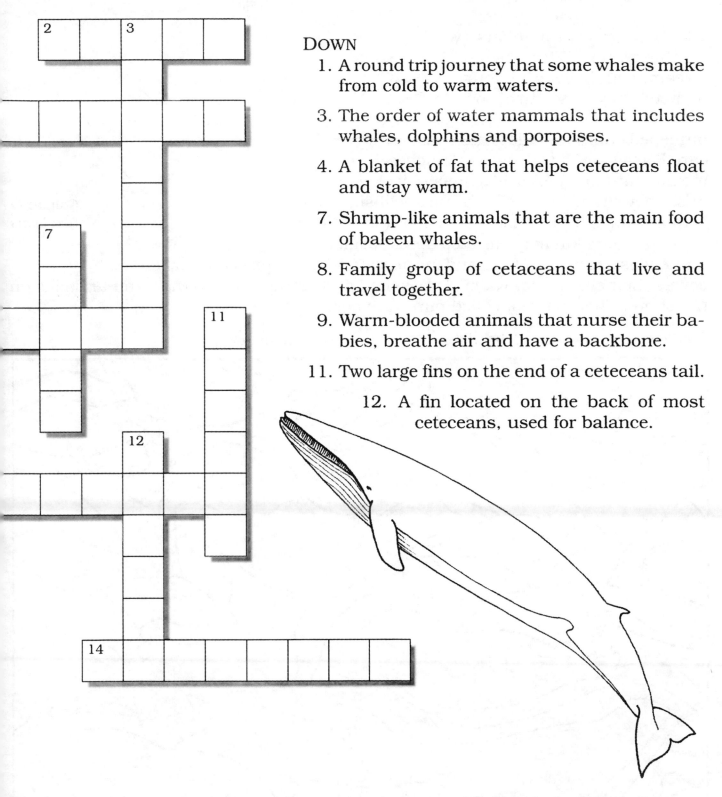

DOWN

1. A round trip journey that some whales make from cold to warm waters.

3. The order of water mammals that includes whales, dolphins and porpoises.

4. A blanket of fat that helps ceteceans float and stay warm.

7. Shrimp-like animals that are the main food of baleen whales.

8. Family group of cetaceans that live and travel together.

9. Warm-blooded animals that nurse their babies, breathe air and have a backbone.

11. Two large fins on the end of a ceteceans tail.

12. A fin located on the back of most ceteceans, used for balance.

WORD LIST: Baleen, Blowhole, Blubber, Cetacean, Dorsal, Echolocation, Flippers, Flukes, Krill, Mammal, Migration, Orcas, Plankton, Pod

PINNEPEDS

Seals are graceful acrobats in the water. With their streamlined body and four flippers, they twist, turn, somersault and glide easily. The pinneped family includes true seals, eared seals and walruses. Pinneped means "fin-footed." A seal's flippers look like fins. They eat all kinds of fish and shellfish, octopus and squid. A thick layer of blubber beneath their skin helps to keep them warm. Pinnepeds see well on land and in the water. A clear protective layer covers their eyes under water. They spend part of their lives in the water and part on the shore. Their babies, called pups, are born on land.

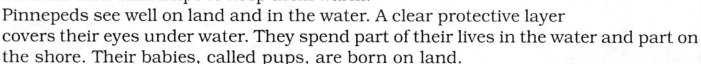

California Sea Lions

Find and color the hidden harbor seals. How many seals are there? _____

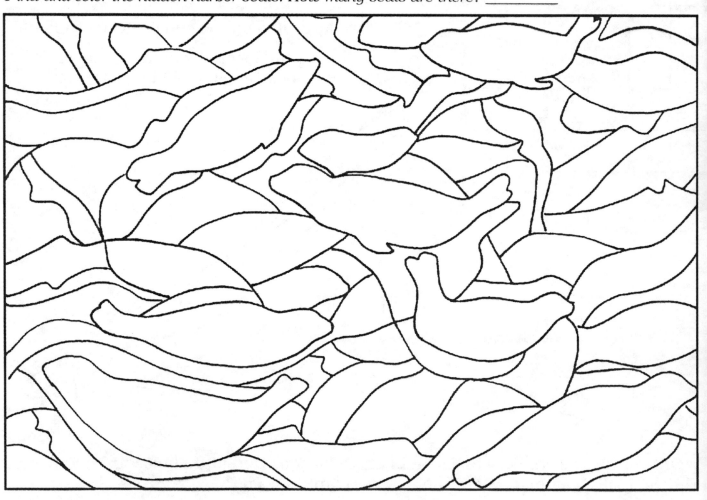

18

HARBOR SEAL: A TRUE SEAL

Harbor seals are the smallest and most commonly seen pinnepeds in Puget Sound. An adult male grows to six feet and weighs 300 pounds. They are earless seals. Harbor seals are often seen in groups swimming with their friends looking for something to eat or resting on rocks, beaches or docks. If you see a baby seal alone, don't worry, the mother will return. She is hunting for food. Please don't try to touch the seals.

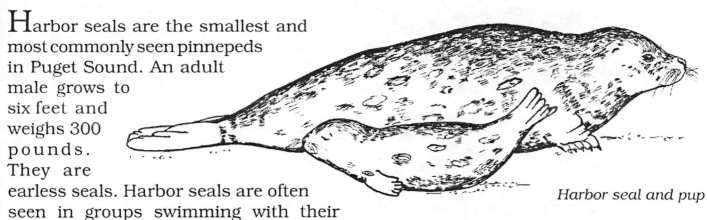

Harbor seal and pup

Harbor seals are easy to identify because they are the only seals in Puget Sound that are spotted. Their hair color ranges from tan to silver to black with white rings.

CALIFORNIA SEA LION: AN EARED SEAL

While out on the water, you may hear loud barking. Don't worry, it's not dogs lost at sea, but a group of California sea lions. They can set up quite a racket next to canneries or fishing boats looking for something to eat. In the last few years, the California sea lion has become a familiar sight in Greater Puget Sound. At the H. M. Chitenden Locks in Seattle, they have become a serious problem. The sea lions eat salmon trying to climb the fish ladder from Puget Sound to Lake Union. California sea lions have small ears and are dark brown or black. The adult males can grow to eight feet long and weigh 600 pounds.

California sea lion

19

TRUE SEALS AND EARED SEALS

True seals, like harbor seals, use their back flippers for swimming. They spread out their webbed flippers and move them in a side-to-side motion.

Eared seals do not use their hind flippers for swimming. They make big sweeping motions with their powerful, front flippers.

True Seal or Eared Seal?

True seals have ears but no visible ear flaps. They cannot use their back flippers on land. They move by bumping along on their bellies and flexing their bodies like a caterpillar. Some true seals use their two short, front flippers to help pull themselves along. Eared seals, like the California sea lion, have obvious ear flaps. They are able to take steps with all four flippers.

SILHOUETTE IDENTIFICATION GAME

Can you identify these Greater Puget Sound animals from their silhouettes? To make it even harder, we have changed their sizes.

MUSTELIDS

Anytime is playtime for the fun-loving otter. One moment it can be looking for food and the next, somersaulting and playing tag with a friend. They are expert swimmers and divers. Otters have thick, dense fur to keep them warm. The under layer of fur traps air and forms an "air barrier" to keep the otter's skin dry. They talk to each other with chirps, squeals, growls and screams.

Otters' toes are webbed for swimming. Their front paws are used to gather and manipulate food. Special valves close their nostrils and ears when they are under the water.

Did You Know?

Did you know that otters belong to the same family as weasels, skunks, ferrets, badgers, wolverines and minks? They are all members of the mustelid family.

RIVER OTTER

The river otter is the most commonly seen otter in the coastal waters of Puget Sound. They can be seen along beaches and shores of quiet streams and waterways. With their sharp teeth they catch fish, mice and other small animals. An adult weighs about 35 pounds and measures up to 4 1/2 feet. River otters generally do not build their own homes. They nest in thick shrubs or caves. Sometimes they even borrow a den from another animal.

21

RIVER OTTER MATCH-UP

Otters are curious fellows. To observe their surroundings, they are able to stand upright by using their tail as a prop. These 6 river otters look very similar, but only two are exactly alike. Can you find the two that match?

River otters are excellent swimmers and divers and can stay underwater for up to five minutes. They paddle with all four feet, using their tail as a rudder. By tucking in their feet and undulating their body, somewhat like the human butterfly stroke, they can swim up to seven miles an hour.

SEA OTTER

Sea otters are a cousin to the river otter. They are the largest of the mustelid family and can weigh up to 100 pounds and measure five feet long. Sea otters like to swim on their backs and use their hind feet to paddle. They even sleep and eat while lying on their backs. They like to sleep cradles in a bed of kelp.

The sea otter is one of the few mammals that uses tools. Floating on it's back, it places a rock on it's belly, and hits the shellfish against it, breaking open the shell. Abalones, clams, crabs, fish and mussels, octopus, squid and sea urchins are their favorite foods. A sea otter often has a favorite rock which it carries in a fold of skin under his arm. Although sea otters spend most of their time in the water, they do not have blubber to keep them warm. Instead, they have thick, dense fur.

During the 18th and 19th centuries, sea otters were hunted almost to extinction in the Puget Sound area because of their beautiful fur. Efforts to halt the hunting of sea otters and transplanting them back to their original homes have been encouraging. They are now seen on the outer coast of Washington, but are still rarely seen in Greater Puget Sound.

River Otter or Sea Otter?

River otters are much smaller than sea otters. They have brown coats and long slender tails. Sea otters have brown coats with gray faces and thicker, shorter tails. Sea otters eat and swim on their backs, generally river otters do not. Sea otters' back feet are flipper-like, river otters' are not. You may see river otters on a docks or beaches but sea otters are rarely seen on land.

PACIFIC SALMON

Don't tell a Pacific salmon you can't go home again!

Pacific salmon are born in fresh water streams and return to spawn and die there, but they live most of their lives in the salty waters of the ocean thousands of miles from their birthplace.

Life begins for the Pacific salmon in fresh water streams or rivers. In the fall, the females bury their eggs in gravel. In the spring they hatch and are called "alevins." These worm-like fish are less than an inch long. They are nourished by yolk sac that are attached to their stomachs. After they use up their yolk sacs they move into deeper water. They are called "fry" as they begin to swim, feeding on smaller animals and insects. The fry can spend weeks or years in the waters where they are born. When the salmon begin to migrate to the ocean, they are called "smolts." Their trip can be as long as 2,000 miles.

When they are ready to spawn, after one to seven years, an internal clock tells the salmon to head for the river or stream where they were born. They follow chemical clues and smells to find their way. Some scientists believe they also "read" the location

The panels of this story are mixed up. Can you unscramble the pictures so they tell the story of the life cycle of the Pacific Salmon? Number the boxes 1 to 6, beginning with the spawning salmon.

SMOLTS

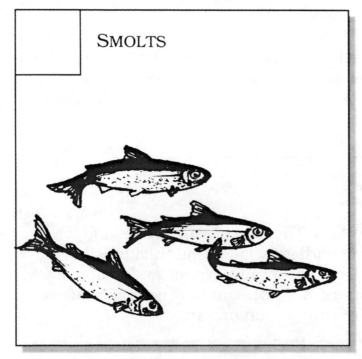

FRY

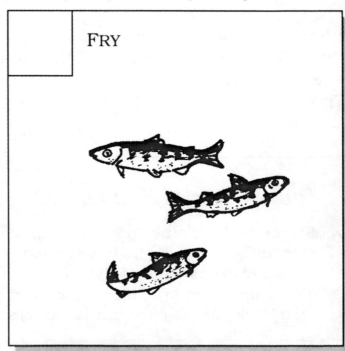

of the sun and stars to chart their journey.

When the salmon re-enter fresh water, they begin changing physically. Their colors change from silver to red or black or green. The male develops a hooked nose and a hump on his back. The female grows fat with eggs. When they reach their birthplace, the female lays her eggs in the gravel and the male fertilizes them. Within two weeks the male and female die. The life cycle of the salmon begins again when the eggs hatch in the spring.

ALEVINS

EGGS

SPAWNING

RETURNING

OTHER FISH

There are many kinds of fish that live in the saltwater of Greater Puget Sound. Different kinds of fish require different combinations of light, water temperature, water current, oxygen content, and food to survive. These differences help them avoid direct competition with each other.

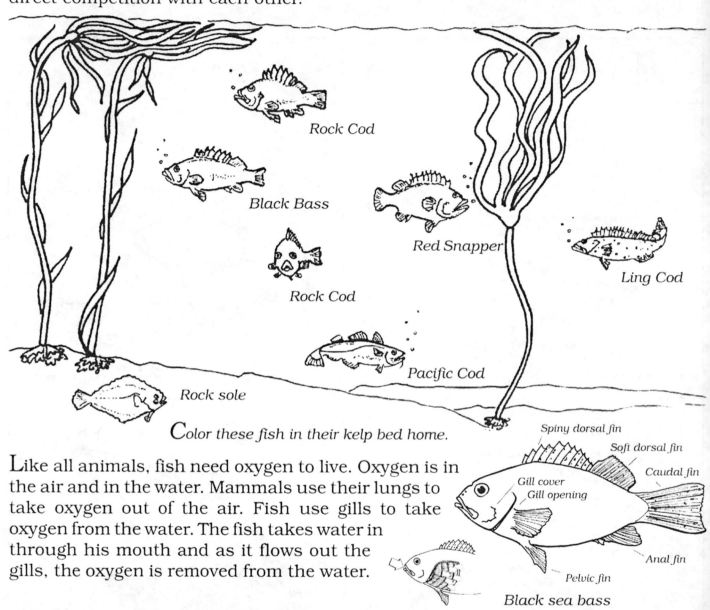

Rock Cod

Black Bass

Red Snapper

Rock Cod

Ling Cod

Pacific Cod

Rock sole

Color these fish in their kelp bed home.

Spiny dorsal fin

Soft dorsal fin

Caudal fin

Gill cover
Gill opening

Anal fin

Pelvic fin

Black sea bass

Like all animals, fish need oxygen to live. Oxygen is in the air and in the water. Mammals use their lungs to take oxygen out of the air. Fish use gills to take oxygen from the water. The fish takes water in through his mouth and as it flows out the gills, the oxygen is removed from the water.

When is a Fish not a Fish?

When it is a jellyfish, starfish or shellfish. These animals do not have backbones and so are not fish. All fish have a backbone, use gills to breathe oxygen and are cold-blooded.

26

OCTOPUS: A SHY GUY

Have you heard old stories of "devilfish" or octopuses attacking men at sea and sailing ships? Actually octopuses are shy, gentle animals and avoid contact with any large animal. They live alone in caves, under rocks and other dark spots. In fact, sometimes they make their own caves by piling up rocks, bottles or old tires.

Octopuses are *Cephalopods*, meaning animals that have a beaked mouth, an internal shell, large brains and long flexible arms. They are mollusks, like clams, oysters and snails, but many cephalopods have lost their outside shell. Other cephalopods are squid, cuttlefish, and the chambered nautilus. Octopuses are unusual because they have no shells or bones.

They are strange looking animals with a soft, bag-shaped body, protruding eyes and eight arms. The body and head are one unit and it is covered by a thick outer muscle and skin called the mantle. Their yellow eyes stand up on rounded knobs and provide a full 360 degree range of vision. They use their mouth, or beak, to break through shellfish and mollusks, which are their primary food. The mouth is hidden on the underside and is surrounded by what look like arms, called tentacles. Each of their eight tentacles has about 240 discs, which work like suction cups.

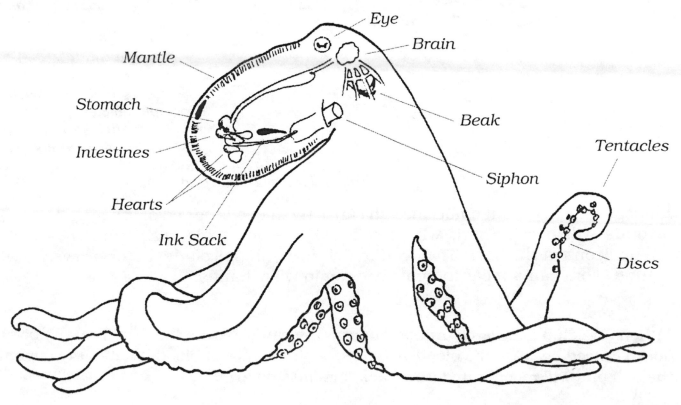

27

OCTOPUS

Octopuses swim by gently drawing water into their mantle and pushing water out through their siphon. The force of the water can move the octopus as fast as 8 miles per hour. Frightened octopuses can shoot out a brown, inky liquid as they speed away from their enemies. Actually, octopuses do not normally swim, but prefer to travel by pulling themselves along using the suction cups on their tentacles.

Because they have no bones, octopuses can change their shape. To escape an enemy, they can become big and round or long and thin. They can easily slip into holes and cracks and crawl under rocks. Octopuses camouflage themselves to hide from predators, changing their color and skin texture. When on the dark ocean floor they turn brown, when they swim through eel grass, they turn green, in very blue water, they turn blue. Against a bumpy surface their skin appears knobby and against a flat surface their skin is smooth.

Frightened octopuses can shoot out a brown, black or purple inky liquid as they speed away from their enemies. The ink not only clouds the predator's vision but can act as a decoy. When the octopus mixes his ink with mucous, the ink is shaped like the octopus. While the predator tries to capture the inky cloud, the real octopus gets away. Color the octopus and its ink.

Biologists believe that emotions can cause them to change color; an angry or excited octopus will become red, whereas he will become pale with fear. They are the "chameleons of the sea." They can match a rusting airplane motor or even a white plate. Colors can appear in spots or even in wavy bands.

When an octopus severely injures an arm, he can separate his arm from his body. It doesn't bleed because his blood vessels seal off the flow of blood. In about two months the octopus will regenerate (grow back) his missing arm.

28

What are 3 things an octopus can do to hide from an enemy?

1. _____

2. _____

3. _____

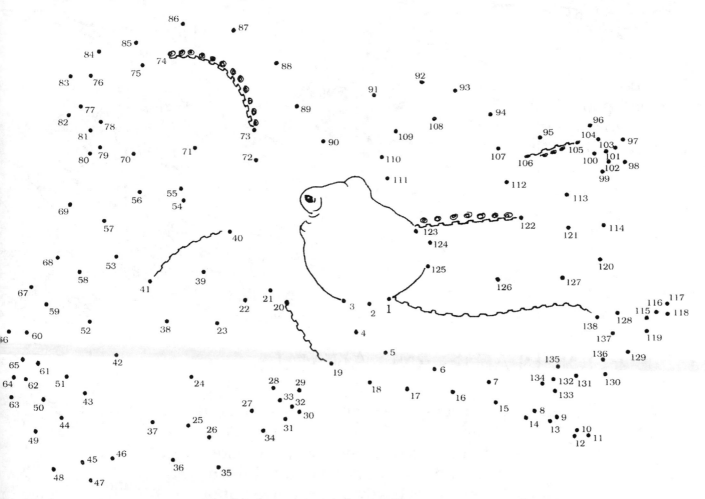

Connect the dots in order from 1 to 138 to complete the picture of the Giant Pacific Octopus. Decide where he is hiding. What color is he?

Where are the Largest Octopuses in the World?

The largest octopuses in the world live in Puget Sound. The Giant Pacific Octopus can weigh as much as 125 pounds and has an arm (tenacle) span of twenty feet.

THE ROCKY TIDE POOL

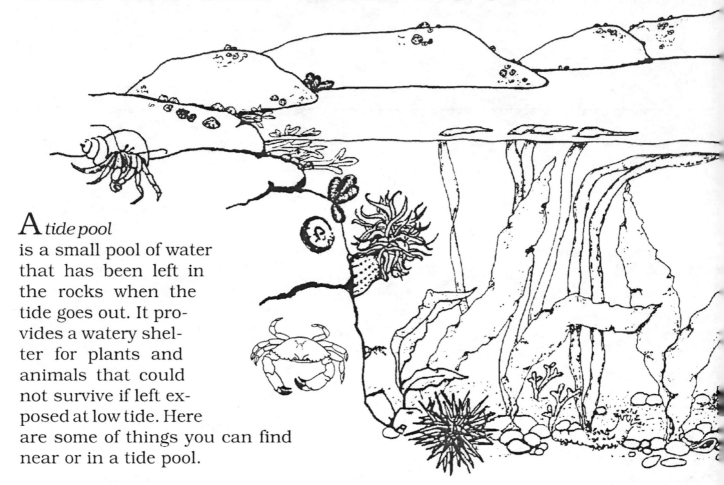

A *tide pool* is a small pool of water that has been left in the rocks when the tide goes out. It provides a watery shelter for plants and animals that could not survive if left exposed at low tide. Here are some of things you can find near or in a tide pool.

TIDE POOL PLANTS AND ANIMALS

The rocks are covered with *seaweeds* of all colors, shapes and sizes. They are anchored to the rocks by pads called holdfasts. The green and brown seaweeds are hardy and can live out of the water for short periods of times. The red seaweeds are the most fragile and live in the deepest water.

Bull kelp

Alaria

Sea lettuce

Clinging to shoreline rocks or dock pilings, you might see clusters of blue-black bivalves called *mussels*. They hang on by strong threads that are spun by a special gland in the foot. The shells, or valves are the outside skeleton of the mussel. Protected inside the shell is the soft bodied mussel. Like most bivalves they are filter feeders, using their gills to draw in water and food.

Mussels

30

Using the correct colors, color the plants and animals you find in the tide pool and on the rocks.

Periwinkle

Limpets, whelks and *periwinkles* are members of the snail family. They have one shell and are called univalves. Their foot has a hard bony plate that acts like a trap door. It protects the animals from their enemies and keeps water inside the shell while they are left dry at low tide.

Limpits

Limpits have cone-shaped shells. Sometimes people call them Chinese hats. The are generally brown with flecks or bands of white. The shells of the wrinkled

Whelks

whelks and periwinkles are curved into a spiral. The shells of whelks are bumpy and sometimes very beautiful. The periwinkle shell is smooth and varies in color from dark brown to almost white, with bands of yellow or orange. Periwinkles, whelks and limpits cling to rocks by a foot that acts like a suction cup. They eat algae and small seaweeds. Look around them and see where they have eaten whole patches of aglae off the rocks. During the day they stay in one place, but at night or high tide they move around and graze on algae. No one knows how they do it but they always return to the same spot and even lie pointing in the same direction.

31

MORE ROCKY TIDE POOL ANIMALS

Barnacles are animals that stand on their head and eat with their feet. They attach their heads to solid objects like rocks, pilings and even other sea animals. When barnacles want to eat, they sticks out their feather-like feet and brush tiny animals into their mouths.

Barnacles

The *chiton*, pronounced ki-ton, clings tightly to the rocks with its foot. Instead of one shell like the limpit, it has eight interlocking plates that overlap like shingles on a roof. If taken off of a rock, they curl up in a ball to protect their soft body. They can grow as long as six inches and are usually the color of the rock they occupy. They graze on algae during the night or at high tide and always return to the same spot.

Chiton

The *sea anenome* looks more like a flower than an animal. They vary in color, being green, blue, yellow, pink, orange or red and sometimes even a combination of colors. The colorful "petals" are really poisonous tentacles. When an anemone is hungry, the tentacles reach out to sting and paralyze their prey, such as small fish, crab or shrimp. The tentacle drags the food into the anenome's mouth which is located in the central "stem". They eat their food whole, and spit out the shells they cannot digest. At low tide, or when disturbed, the anenome pulls in its tentacles and shortens its body, looking like a jelly-like lump on a rock. Most anenomes stay on the same rock their whole life, but some others slide on their muscular bases.

Sea anemones

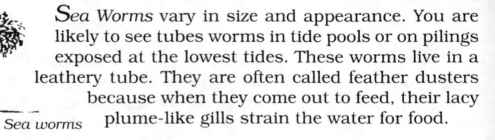

Sea Worms vary in size and appearance. You are likely to see tubes worms in tide pools or on pilings exposed at the lowest tides. These worms live in a leathery tube. They are often called feather dusters because when they come out to feed, their lacy plume-like gills strain the water for food.

Sea worms

If you find an animal that looks a lot like a flat, dill pickle, it is a *sea cucumber*. It has red, orange, brown or purple leathery skin with five rows of tube feet down the sides. At one end there

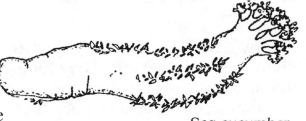

Sea cucumber

is a mouth with tentacles around it. The tentacles are sticky and the cucumber stretches them out to catch small animals. They put their tentacles in their mouth, one by one, scraping off the food. Sea cucumbers have a strange way of avoiding attack. When an enemy approaches, they squirt out part of their insides! While the animal is busy eating, the cucumber escapes. In a short time, it will regrow the part that it has sacrificed.

Sea star

The *sea star* or starfish comes in many shapes, sizes and colors. They are not fish, but members of a group of animals called *echinoderms*, which include sea cucumbers and sea urchins. Their main body is like the hub of a wheel with rays radiating like spokes from the center. The suction-like tube feet are used for moving, feeding, breathing and sensing. The mouth and stomach are located on the underside, in the the center of the body. Sea stars have at least five rays. The sunflower star, perhaps the largest sea star, measures 20 to 30 inches and has 24 or more rays.

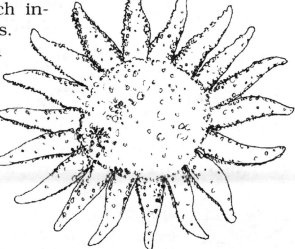

Sunflower star

Sea urchin

Sea urchins look like colored pincushions and feel like it too! Their shell, called a *test*, is almost as round as a ball. The fragile shell is covered with bands of spines that protect them from enemies. Between their spiny bands are five double rows of tube feet which they use to move. Sea urchins cannot live out of the water. You may find their fragile, white, empty shells on the beach. There are red, green and purple sea urchins in the Puget Sound area. Like their close relative the sea star, their mouths are on the bottom of their body. They eat mostly seaweeds, especially bull kelp, and small animals like barnacles.

EVEN MORE ROCKY TIDE POOL ANIMALS

Many small fish are trapped in tide pools when the tide goes out. They hide in seaweed, cracks in rocks or bury themselves in the sand. The most common tide pool fish is the *blenny*. They average about three inches long, are green and brownish and resemble an eel. The black, brown and green *sculpin* blends into the rocks and seaweeds of the tide pool. You can identify them from their big heads and narrow bodies. They grow to about four inches long.

Sculpin

Blenny

What animal looks like a transparent umbrella with streamers? The *jellyfish*. They aren't really a fish at all, they have no fins, scales or bones. These unusual animals are made mostly of water. Their bodies have a mouth and stomach, but no brain, eyes or ears. The streamers are actually arms and tentacles covered with stinging cells. They swim by opening and closing their umbrella-like body, their tentacles floating behind searching for food. The jellyfish use their tentacles to paralyze small animals and bring the food to their mouth, which is located in the center of their body. You are likely to see the small transparent Moon Jellyfish in quiet bays or stranded in a tide pool.

Moon jellyfish

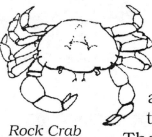

Crabs are one of the most interesting creatures you will find. They are a member of the *Crustacean* family. Crustaceans have two pairs of antenna, jointed limbs and an outer shell that protects their body. As crabs grow, they shed their old shells. They hide in crevices or under seaweeds waiting for their new shell to harden. There are many kinds of crabs but the ones you are most likely to find at low tide are the rock crabs, hermit crabs and Dungeness crabs.

Rock Crab

Hermit crab

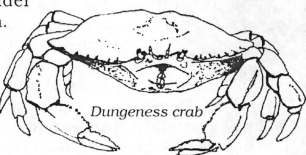
Dungeness crab

Try looking under some rocks for some small rock crabs. After looking at them, be sure to replace the rocks as you don't want to disturb their home.

ANIMAL DEFENSES

Nature can seem cruel, with some animals preying on other animals. Many animals have developed behaviors that protect themselves from predators.

Describe what these animals do to protect themselves.

Sea cucumbers _____

Octopus _____

Limpets _____

Blennies or sculpins _____

Crabs _____

Chitons _____

ANIMAL CLOSE-UPS

Here are 6 close-up pictures of tide pool animals that you have studied. Can you tell what they are?

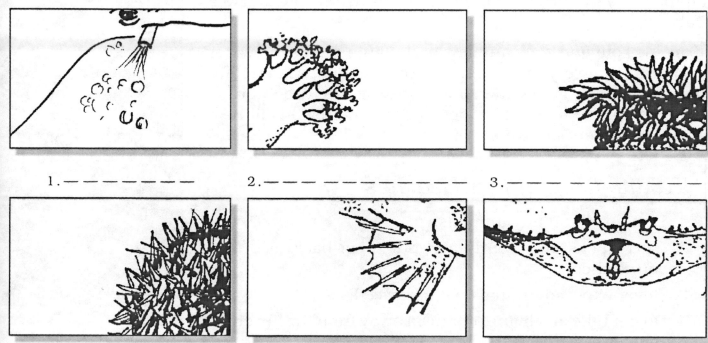

1. _ _ _ _ _ _

2. _ _ _ _ _ _ _ _ _

3. _ _ _ _ _ _ _ _

4. _ _ _ _ _ _ _

5. _ _ _ _ _ _

6. _ _ _ _

TIDE ZONES

Have you noticed that the water level in Puget Sound changes during the day? It is affected by the gravitational pull of the moon and sun. The water level changes twice a day with the rise and fall of the tide. Marine biologists have divided the beach into *tide zones* depending on the time it is covered with water. Here is a list of the tide zones of Puget Sound, with some plant and animal inhabitants.

Zone 1. The *splash zone* is the highest on the beach. It is dry except during a storm or a very high tide. Here you may find yellow Sea Hair, blue-green algae, periwinkles and sand louse.

Zone 2. In the *high tide zone* you may find barnacles, limpets and rock crabs. Olive-green Rock Weed and bright green Sea Lettuce are seaweeds that live here. These animals and plants require time out of the water. The tide brings their food to them with the incoming water.

Zone 3. The *middle tide zone* is generally covered and uncovered twice a day with water. Animals and plants found here require some time each day to be exposed to the air. Here you may find blue mussels, purple sea stars, anenomes, black chitons and wrinkled whelks. Temperatures do not change very much, so here the olive-brown Sea Sac and Sea Palm grow.

Zone 4. *Low tide zone* animals and plants are in the water except during very low tides. Red sea urchins, sea cucumbers, sun stars, green anenomes, brittle stars, tube worms, Dungeness and kelp crabs, octopuses and brown Bull Kelp and Red Eyelet Silk live in this zone.

Sargassum

Taking Care of Our Beaches

1. Don't walk on any animals.
2. Turn rocks over gently and put them back as you found them.
3. Cover exposed animals with seaweed.
4. Do not take any living organism away from the beach.
5. Fill in any holes you dig.

Do You Know What Makes a Wave?

Most waves are caused by wind blowing over the top of the water. As the wind blows, it creates small ripples. The more the wind blows, the larger the waves.

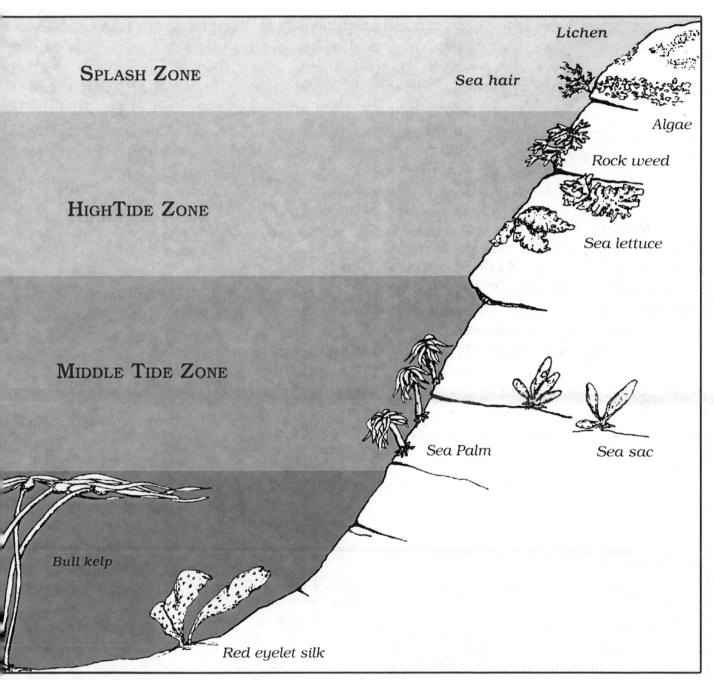

SPLASH ZONE

HIGH TIDE ZONE

MIDDLE TIDE ZONE

Lichen

Sea hair

Algae

Rock weed

Sea lettuce

Sea Palm

Sea sac

Bull kelp

Red eyelet silk

Can you draw some of the animals you have learned about? Here is a picture of the beach with the tide zones marked. Draw and color the animals you might see in the tide zone where they live.

SEA GULL

The first birds to welcome you to the seashore are sea gulls. Although there are many different kinds of gulls in the Puget Sound area, the Glaucous-winged Gull is the most commonly seen. Young birds have streaked gray-brown and white feathers with a dark bill. By the time they are four years old, most gulls are white bodied with pearl-gray backs and wings. They have a yellow bill with a red spot. With a wingspan of 23-25 inches, gulls can glide on currents of air called updrafts. In a strong updraft, they can appear motionless. Gulls may travel at 25 miles per hour. Unlike most birds, gulls have waterproof feathers and webbed feet.

Sea gulls are scavengers who will eat anything they can find: insects, dead animals or fish, garbage or any "hand-out." Like meat-eating birds, the gull's beak has a hook at the end. This helps them hold their food and pull it apart. Sometimes you can watch sea gulls fly up and drop clams and other shellfish onto rocks and even roads. This breaks open the shell so the sea gull can eat the meat inside. Sea gulls are never content to eat alone; they can be heard calling their friends to come join the feast.

Sea gulls use seaweed, kelp and grass to make their nests. They nest in colonies on isolated rocky cliffs and grassy slopes.

38

BALD EAGLE

Bald eagles are the most powerful and magnificient birds of Greater Puget Sound. Although they may look bald, they are not really bald. Snowy white feathers on the head and neck of adult bald eagles make them look bald. Their tails are white and the wings and body are dark brown. Eagles under 5 years have dark brown feathers with scattered white markings. The male and female have the same coloring, but the female is slightly larger. Each year they get a new coat of feathers. When grown they weigh about 12 pounds and have a wingspan of six to eight feet across. Young eagles become partners for life. Eagles live 20 to 30 years.

Bald Eagles are great fishermen. When an eagle sees a fish near the surface of the water, it flies down with its sharp claws extended and snatches the fish. Their favorite food is fish but they also eat small birds and animals and even garbage.

They build their stick nests, called eyries, in the tops of tall trees, near the water. Their nests are often huge; some have measured 10 feet across and 20 feet deep. When ready to nest, a pair of eagles will return to the same eyrie. Each year they add new sticks and other building material, such as bark, moss, grass and sometimes even dirt, to their eyrie.

Have you heard the phrase, "He has an eagle eye?" Some scientists believe eagles have better eyesight than any other animal. Their eyes are so sharp some eagles can see a fish from almost a mile away.

The bald eagle is only found in North America and is the national bird of the United States. The bald eagle is an endangered species. Many of their nesting areas are being destroyed. The toxic chemicals in the fish and animals they eat are harming their ability to reproduce.

GREAT BLUE HERON

The Great Blue Heron is the big long-legged, long-necked bird you see standing along rocky shores or fishing in a shallow bay. It really isn't blue, but gray with a white head and black plumes. Standing about four feet tall and with a wingspan of seven feet, it is the largest heron in North America. They make a hoarse croaking sound and, when frightened, their squawks sound pre-historic.

Herons are not fussy eaters, they eat fish, frogs, snakes, small birds and animals. To hunt, the heron stands motionless in shallow water. When its prey comes within striking distance, their sharp bill stabs with lightning speed. Even though herons have a narrow bill and slender neck they are able to swallow, head first, a 12-inch fish!

Great Blue Herons usually nest in colonies called rookeries, located in secluded woods close to water. Their stick nests are built in tall trees and are about three feet wide. The inside of the nest is lined with twigs, moss, lichens or conifer needles. The male and female couple work together to build their nest. Sometimes they build new nests, but often restore old ones. Rookeries can vary in size from two to several hundred nests.

40

The heron makes a spectacular show as it spreads its wings and soars, making slow, deep wing movements. In flight, a heron holds its long neck folded back onto its shoulders, forming an S-curve, its long legs trailing.

ESCAPE MAZE

The Great Blue Heron is looking for his dinner. Help the fish escape to the rock cave.

ANIMAL CROSSWORD

Using the pictures below as clues, fill in this animal crossword puzzle.

3. (orca)
7. (whale)
11. (eagle)

4. (crab)
8. (clam)
12. (nudibranch)
15. (seal)
18. (flounder)

1. (heron)
5. (snail)
9. (starfish)
13. (octopus)
16. (bird on post)
19. (sea lion)

2. (otter)
6. (sea urchin)
10. (salmon)
14. (jellyfish)
17. (bean/egg)

In the picture below, can you find the 15 hidden objects? Find the fishhook, cane, eyeglasses, cup, comb, toes, paint brush, umbrella, bowling pin, banana, sewing needle, pencil, feather, heart and diamond ring.

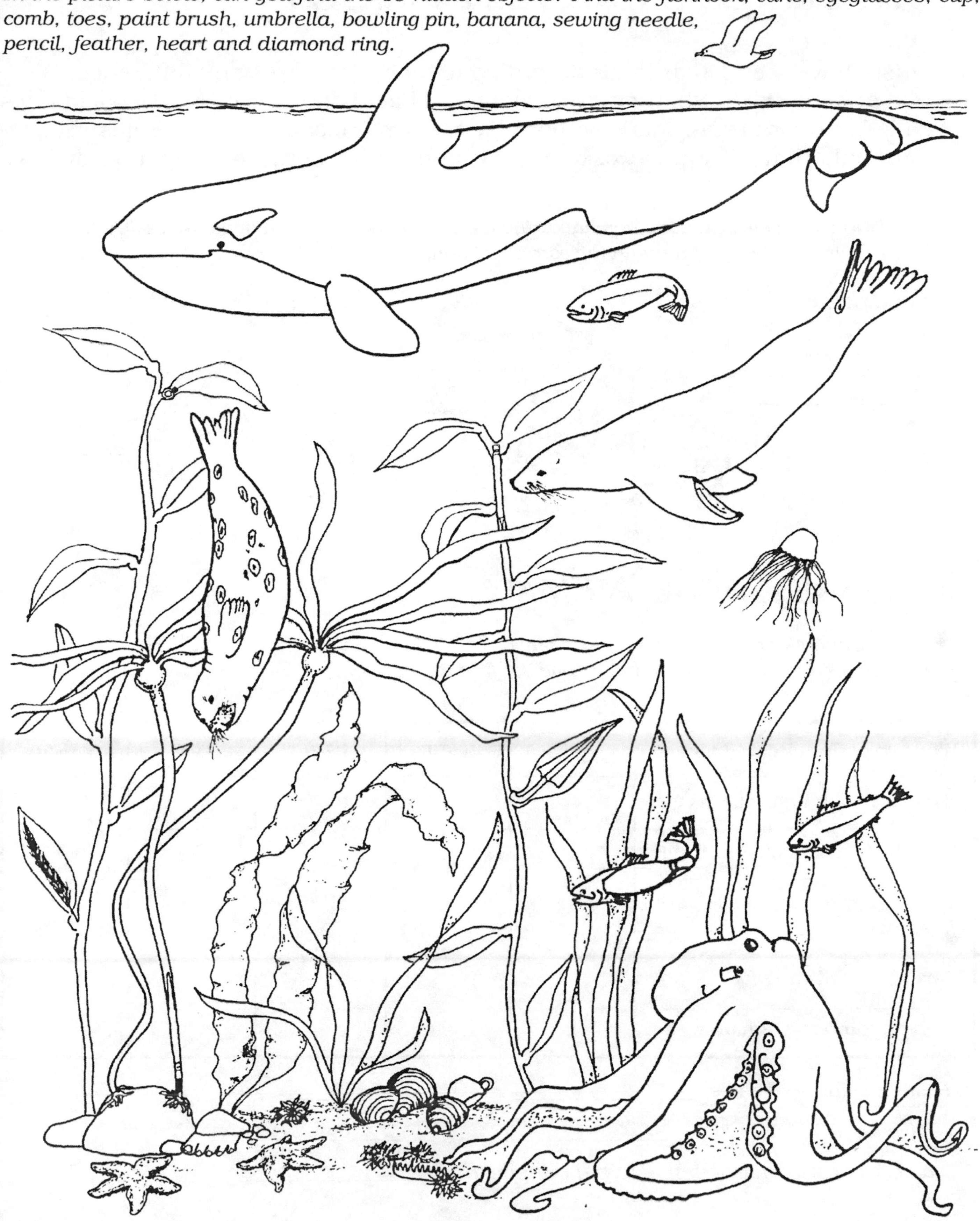

VERTEBRATES AND INVERTEBRATES

Scientists have grouped animals according to their likenesses and differences. One method of grouping is whether an animal has a backbone. Animals with backbones are called *vertebrates*. Animals without backbones are called *invertebrates*. Generally, animals that have an *exoskeleton* (a hard, outer body covering) do not have backbones.

Pictured below are some animals you have studied. Determine which animals are vertebrates and which are invertebrates. List them in the correct column.

Vertebrates Invertebrates

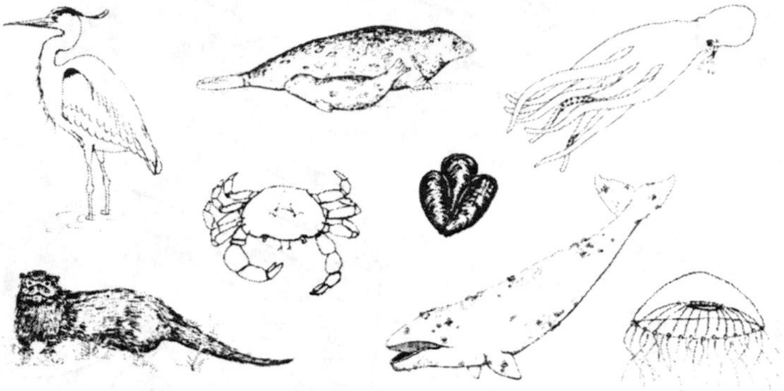

_____   _____

_____   _____

_____   _____

_____   _____

COMPARE THESE ANIMALS

These five animals are very different, yet have some things in common. Fill in the chart below and compare their characteristics. We have done the first row for you.

	Salmon	Orca	Eagle	Octopus	Harbor seal
Warm-blooded or cold-blooded	cold	warm	warm	cold	warm
Born alive or hatched from eggs					
Breathes through gills or lungs					
Types of appendages (*flippers, fins, wings, tentacles*)					
Parent feeds young (*yes or no*)					
Habitat (*air, land or water*)					

1. Name the two mammals. _____ _____

2. Which animals have gills? _____ _____

3. Name a hatched animal that is fed by the parents. _____

WHAT DO THESE ANIMALS EAT?

Draw line connecting these animals with the things they eat. The first one has been done for you.

WHERE IS MY HOME?

The area that an animal lives is called a *habitat*. Animals choose a habitat where there is plenty of food for them to eat and they are safe from their enemies.

Draw a line connecting these animals with their home.

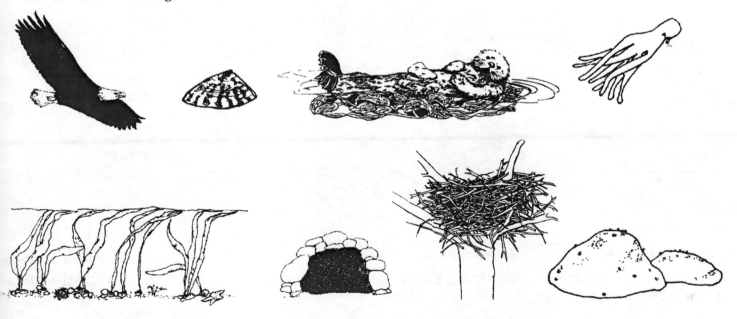

REBUS PUZZLE

Rebus means words by pictures. What words do these pictures spell?

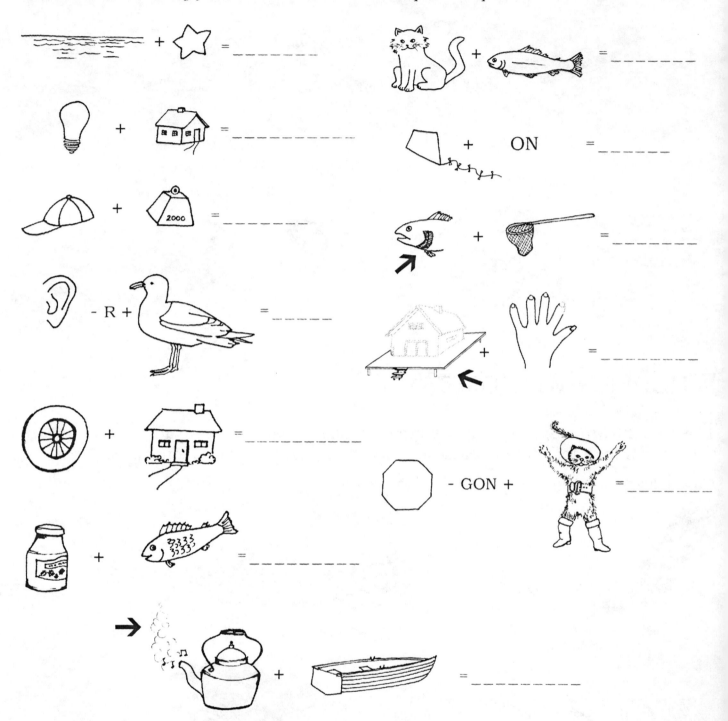

WORD LIST
Sea Star, Lighthouse, Captain, Eagle, Steamboat, Jellyfish, Deckhand, Wheelhouse, Octopus, Chiton, Gillnet.

Boats of Puget Sound

Tug Boat and Barge

The small but mighty tug boat is a common sight on the waters of Puget Sound. Most tugs are 65 feet to 100 feet long. Some tug boat engines are rated at 3,500 horsepower. With its small size and big engine it is used to tow or push large ocean going ships and barges. Tugs are able to work in very bad weather.

Purse Seiner

A seiner is a boat that uses a purse seine net to catch fish. Seine boats usually have a keel length of slightly under 50 feet and are crewed by 5 to 7 men. Salmon seine nets may be 1,800 feet long. Fishermen use seine nets to catch schools of fish that swim near the surface, fish like salmon and herring. The nets have floats along the top with weights and rings attached to the bottom edge. A rope called a *purse line* runs through the rings. When a school of fish is seen, a small power boat called a skiff, is released. The net is set in a circle around the fish. The crew on the boat's deck then pulls in the purse line, capturing the fish in the "purse" of the net.

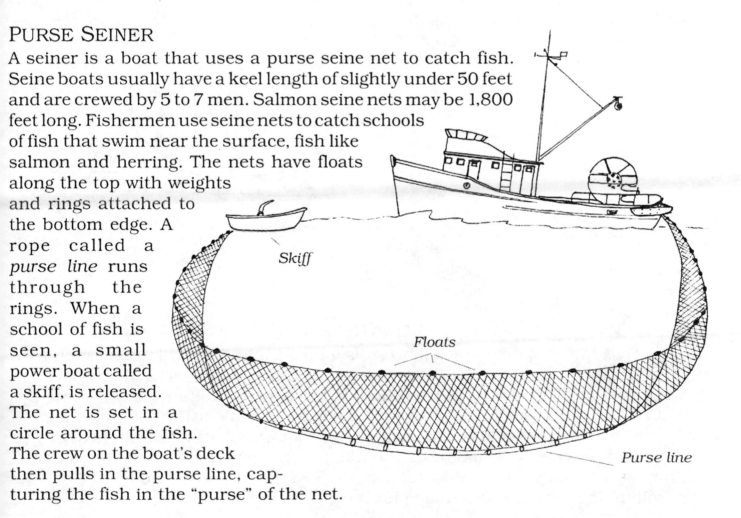

Skiff

Floats

Purse line

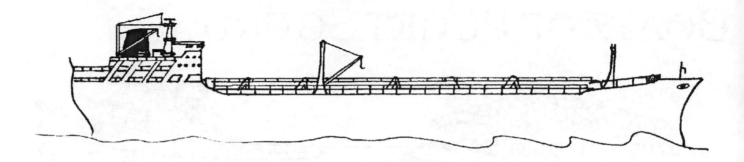

FREIGHTERS AND TANKERS

Freighters and tankers are the largest ships in Puget Sound. You are most likely to see freighters, carrying general cargo or logs, and oil tankers. Freighters come from all over the world for import and export of goods. Tankers are made to carry liquid cargo. They generally carry oil but sometimes carry other liquid chemicals. The largest ships allowed on Puget Sound must be under 1,000 feet in length with a dead weight of no more than 125,000 tons.

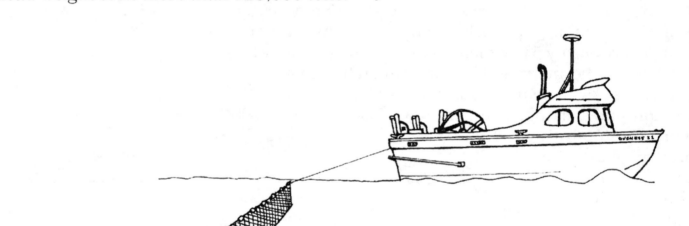

GILL NETTER

A gill netter is a boat that uses a gill net to catch fish. The boats are run by one or two men. The boats are generally less than 50 feet long. Gill nets are long rectangular nets with floats on top and weights along the bottom. They can be 1,800 feet in length. The net forms a wall that catches the fish by their gills as they swim into it. The fisherman may catch salmon, bottom fish or even sharks. Most gill netters use a drum wheel to pull in the net. As they roll up the net, the fishermen pick out the fish.

BUOYS

 *Nun buoy*  *Bell buoy* 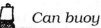 *Can buoy*

You may see some strange shaped objects floating in the water. They are called buoys *(boo-ees)* and are held by anchors. They are shaped and colored to help boaters find their way through waterways. Buoys are also used to warn boaters of rocky areas and shallow waters.

Graceful sailboats and power boats are familiar sights, cruising through the waters of Greater Puget Sound.

BOAT SCRAMBLE PUZZLE

Unscramble the name of each boat below and write it in the numbered box. When you are finished, read down the shaded column to find the name of an animal that eats shellfish.

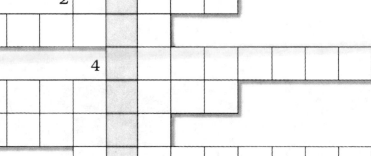

1. reeruspesni

2. refry

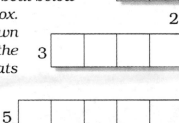

4. bslatoia

5. enlrtgitle

6. beawptroo

3. goubta

7. rigfrteeh

WASHINGTON FERRIES

A visit to Washington would not be complete without a ride on a state ferry. While riding across the icy waters of Puget Sound, you will have an opportunity to see many beautiful places and an abundance of wildlife.

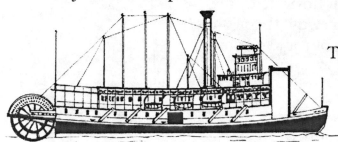

The first ferries were very different from the ones you see today. One early ferry was a wooden, stern-wheeler steamboat. Today there are 21 ferries in the Washington state ferry fleet; it is the largest fleet in the United States. They range in size from the 200 passenger, 34-car *Hiyu* to the Jumbo Mark II, *Tacoma* which carries 2,500 passengers and 202 cars.

The Ferry Captain has a message for you using Morse Code. Using the chart below, decode his message.

- - - - / / - - - / / - - - / / - - - - / / - - -

/ / - - - / / - - - / / - - - / / - / / - - -

/ / - - / / - - - - - / /

Here are the Morse Code signals for the alphabet. Can you send a message to a friend using this code?

A • –	G – – •	M – –	S • • •		
B – • • •	H • • • •	N – •	T –		
C – • – •	I • •	O – – –	U • • –	Y – • – –	
D – • •	J • – – –	P • – – •	V • • • –	Z – – • •	
E •	K – • –	Q – – • –	W • – –	/ Between letters	
F • • – •	L • – • •	R • – •	X – • • –	// Between words	

50

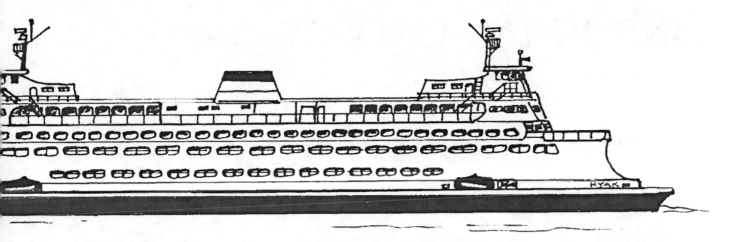

Boat Game Challenge

Can you move 2 ferry boats so that no 2 ferry boats are in the same line horizontally, vertically or diagonally? Circle the boats that need to be moved. Hint: Switch the ferry boats with a fishing boat.

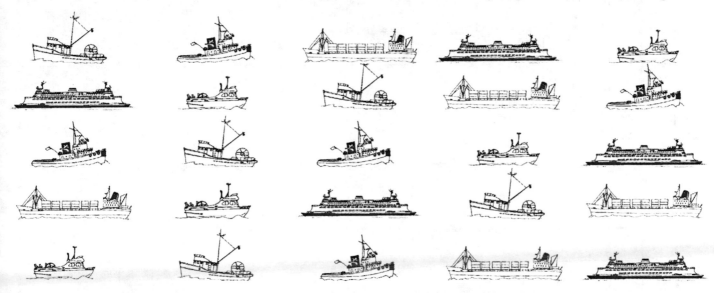

Here are 6 pictures of the ferry Defiance, built in 1927. Although they look very similar, only 2 are exactly alike. Can you find the 2 that match?

ONE FINAL CROSSWORD

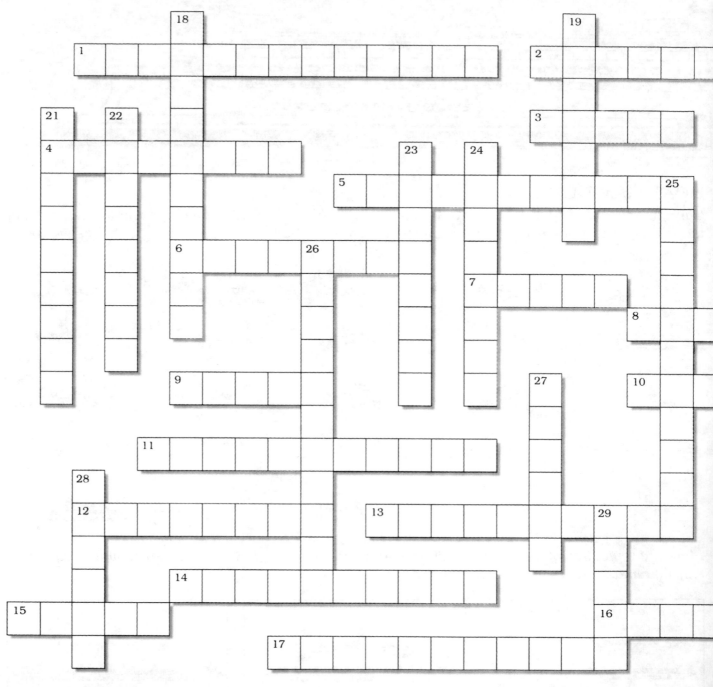

LIST OF CLUES

Barnacle

Buoys

Bivalves

Cephalopod

Cetacean

Chiton

Crabs

Eyries

Exoskeleton

Gills

Gillnetter

Habitat

Harborseals

Holdfast

Invertebrate

Limpit

Mantle

Mussels

Mustelids

Pinneped

Predator

River Otter

Salmon

Sea Cucumber

Tides

Tug boat

Univalve

Vertebrates

Warmblooded

Whelk

ACROSS

1. Animals with no backbones.

2. Layer of skin that covers the body and head of an octopus.

3. Fish use _____ to take oxygen out of the water.

4. Snail family having one shell.

5. Animals with backbones.

6. "Fin-footed" animal.

7. Marine animals with antenna, jointed limbs and exoskeletons.

8. Blue black bi-valves.

9. A wrinkled uni-valve with a bony plate on its foot that acts like a trap door.

10. Power boat used to tow or push ships and barges.

11. An animal that maintains a constant body temperature.

12. Some seaweeds are anchored to rocks by a pad called a _____.

13. The most commonly seen mustelid in the waters of Puget Sound.

14. A fishing boat that uses a net to catch fish by their gills.

15. Used to mark waterways.

16. Stick nests of eagles.

17. Earless pinnepeds commonly seen in Puget Sound.

DOWN

18. A class of mollusk with a beaked mouth, internal shell, large brain and long flexible arms.

19. An area where an animal lives.

20. An animal that stands on its head and eats with its feet.

21. Family that includes otters, weasels, skunks ferrets and minks.

22. Animals that have two shells or valves.

23. An animals that hunts other animals is called a _____.

24. A family of mammals that includes whales, dolphins and porpoises.

25. An animal that squirts out part of his insides to escape danger.

26. A hard body covering.

27. A fish that can live in both salt and fresh water.

28. An animal with eight interlocking plates.

29. The gravitational pull of the moon and the sun causes_____

30. Animals sometimes called Chinese hats.

53

MARINE WORD SEARCH

```
J H D I H M C C R T I D E P O O L N N M
A S L A G N R H E T U G B O A T A O Q E
G F E H C A Q L T S C R D N Q I E M I S
B R N A B Q N M T E T I W B Q C S L B I
C G A O U M N G E A E V H U D G R A E O
G A C Y U R M M N W P E E L A S O S L P
D C L S W P C M L E M R L L E E B C K R
G D S R E H H H L E I O K K L A R U N O
I E O C E A A A I D L T M E C C A L I P
L D R F H T A L G N H T P L A U H P W E
F O N E G I H N E O P E L P N C F I I Q
B C M A N F T G E P R R N L R U H N R M
H G A A E I B O I N H C N J A M A M E F
Q N P K F L E J N E O N A Q B B D R P D
I I B N E N B S K J R M O L B E L O O H
M L E N A K U Q E P H F E I K R C W I N
P B N A H N O M P S H S I F Y L L E J O
N Y A L B P Y L N O R E H E U L B B P P
E L G A E D L A B L L U G A E S K U K I
J K N T A O B L I A S U P O T C O T I K
```

Baldeagle   Buoy   Graywhale   Mussel   Purseiner   Seaanenome   Tidepool
Barnacle   Chiton   Harborseal   Octopus   Riverotter   Seacucumber Tubeworm
Blenny   Crab   Jellyfish   Orca   Sailboat   Seagull   Tugboat
Blueheron   Freighter   Limpet   Periwinkle Salmon   Seaurchin   Whelk
Bullkelp   Gillnetter Lingcod   Porpoise   Sculpin   Seaweed

PUGET SOUND BINGO

As you travel through the Puget Sound area, cross out the picture square on your card when you see the object. For example, if you see a ferry boat, cross out the square with a ferry on it.

Here are four Bingo cards, one for each player. The first person to cross out a row of squares diagonally, up and down, or across is the winner.

ANSWER PAGE

Page 16 & 17 Whale Crossword- 1. Migration, 2. Orcas, 3. Cetaceans, 4. Blubber, 5. Plankton, 6. Baleen, 7. Krill, 8. Pod, 9. Mammal, 10. Echolocation, 11. Flukes, 12. Dorsal, 13. Blowhole, 14. Flippers.

Page 22 River Otter Match-up- Otters 3 and 5 are the same.

Page 24 & 35 1. Spawning, 2. Eggs, 3. Alevins, 4. Fry, 5. Smolts, 6. Returning.

Page 29 Camouflage themselves by changing color, texture and shape, shooting out ink, and hiding under rocks and seaweeds.

Page 35 Animal Defenses- Sea cucumbers squirt out part of their body. Octopus ink and camouflage themselves. Limpets cling to rocks. Blennies and sculpins hide in seaweeds and cracks in rocks or bury themselves in the sand. Crabs hide under seaweeds. Chitons cling to rocks or curl up into a ball.
Animal Close-ups- 1. Octopus, 2. Sea cucumber, 3. Sea anenome, 4. Sea urchin, 5. Blenny, 6. Dungeness crab.

Page 42 1. Great Blue Heron, 2. River otter, 3. Orca, 4. Crab, 5. Periwinkle, 6. Sea urchin, 7. Gray whale, 8. Mussels, 9. Sea star, 10. Salmon, 11. Bald eagle, 12. Sea anenome, 13. Octopus, 14. Jellyfish, 15. Harbor seal, 16. Sea gull, 17. Chiton, 18. Flounder, 19. Sea lion.

Page 44 Vertebrates- Great Blue Heron, River otter, Harbor seal, Gray whale. Invertebrates: Octopus, Crab, Mussels, Jellyfish. 1. Orca, Harbor seal, 2. Salmon, Octopus 3. Eagle

Page 50 Look off the port bow. You can see a pod of orcas!

Page 51 Boat Game Challenge - Row 2 Trade positions of ferry and gillnetter. Row 5 Trade positions of gillnetter and ferry.
Defiance Match-up- Ferries number 2 and 6 are the same.

Page 52 & 53 Puget Sound Crossword- 1. Invertebrates, 2. Mantle, 3. Gills, 4. Univalve, 5. Vertebrates, 6. Pinniped, 7. Crabs, 8. Mussels, 9. Whelk, 10. Tugboat, 11. Warmblooded, 12. Holdfast, 13. River Otter, 14. Gillnetter, 15. Buoys, 16. Eyries, 17. Harbor seal, 18. Cephalopod, 19. Habitat, 20. Barnacle, 21. Mustelids, 22. Bivalves, 23. Predator, 24. Cetacean, 25. Sea Cucumber, 26. Exoskeleton, 27. Salmon, 28. Chiton, 29. Tides, 30. Limpets.

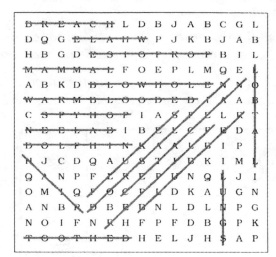

Whale Word Search - Page 6

Salmon	Orca	Eagle	Octopus	Harbor seal
cold	warm	warm	cold	warm
eggs	alive	eggs	eggs	alive
gills	lungs	lungs	gills	lungs
fins	flippers	wings	tentacles	flippers
no	yes	yes	no	yes
water	water	air	water	water

Compare These Animals - Page 44

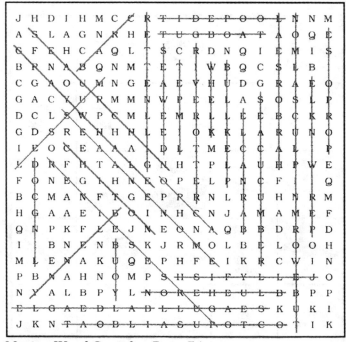

Marine Word Search - Page 54